CHINESE
GARDEN STYLE

For Dominic, Josh, Ferlon, Saffron, Breege, Seth, Simon and Connelia.

CHINESE
GARDEN STYLE

Faith & Geoff Whiten

UNWIN

HYMAN

LONDON SYDNEY WELLINGTON

First published in Great Britain by the Trade Division of Unwin
Hyman Limited, 1988.

UNWIN HYMAN LIMITED
15–17 Broadwick Street
London W1V 1FP

Allen & Unwin Australia Pty Ltd
8 Napier Street, North Sydney, NSW 2060, Australia

Allen & Unwin New Zealand Pty Ltd with the Port Nicholson
Press, 60 Cambridge Terrace, Wellington, New Zealand

ISBN 0 04 440181 7

Designed by Julian Holland

Typeset by MS Filmsetting Limited, Frome, Somerset
Printed in Italy by New Interlitho S.P.A.

Contents

AN IDEA

1 A rainbow on the picturesque
Huangshan Mountain

'Sitting in front of an original ...'

'THE WEST COPIES by sitting in front of a model and imitating it soullessly, outward line by line. When the copy is finished, nothing remains in it of the spirit that had inspired the original. The East "copies" by sitting in front of an original, absorbing it, studying it, grasping its principles and its essential greatness thoroughly; then by going on to translate these acquisitions into a more or less new form, in terms of one's own taste and time, so that another living thing is set moving in the mind, though animated by the same truth that had made the commanding soul of the original. This is rather translation than "copying" as we understand the word; and it is even more indeed than what we mean by translation, for our translations are too often dead renderings from a bygone life; Oriental copying is a perpetual renewal of life, in incessant realisation of its underlying forces, moving perpetually through varying manifestations and developments.'

Reginald Farrer on Rock Gardens and Garden Design, 1912.

In 1986 Queen Elizabeth II was shown by her Chinese hosts around the chambers of the tomb of an Emperor who had ruled their country 2200 years ago. Both Her Majesty's reaction, and that of those who watched on their television screens, was one of complete fascination.

'Another living thing is set moving in the mind.' Reginald Farrer could not possibly have foreseen the enthusiasm with which the West greeted the discovery of the terracotta army of the tomb of Emperor Shihuang-Di, and the curiosity which led people to seek avidly more information about the life of a country that had seemed for so long to be steeped in inscrutable, inaccessible mystery. Yet he was very well aware of the centuries-long love affair of the West with Oriental art and culture, and would have understood those who wanted to see every possible moment of Her Majesty visiting a school to see a children's concert, crossing a lake to have tea in the pavilion that inspired the willow-pattern design, or walking along one small part of the Great Wall, so familiar from childhood encyclopaedias as a tantalizing Wonder of the World.

Gardens were his main preoccupation, and so we hope that Mr Farrer would sympathize with our modern attempt to devise a style that has its source not only in Chinese gardens, but is also inspired by some of the most poignant images of the country held in the Western mind.

IMAGES OF CHINA

2 A lacquered wood screen in twelve folds, with incised and raised ornament painted and gilt on a black background. This dates from the Ch'ing Dynasty and is displayed at the Victoria and Albert Museum.

Before my eyes there is no want of images,
I can stare at patterns kaleidoscopic:
Pearl tassells, kingfisher curtains,
Satin drapes, hibiscus folds,
Scented smoke pours from windows,
The setting sun slants across stairs,
Sun rays depart slower and slower.
Seasonal blooms surround me here:
Peach blossom pink like dots,
Willow leaves tangled like silk thread,
Silken twigs twist toward darkening light,
Shadows fall, dark shades lengthen.

Mosaic by Hsaio Kang

A traditional willow pattern
design.

'A living thing set moving in the mind . . .'

THE ORIENTAL department of Liberty's famous London store is a veritable treasure chest of art, ornaments and bric-à-brac. A taste of China is not expensive: you can buy silk boxes, painted dishes and tea sets, elaborately embroidered cushions, fans, dragon kites, carved camphor wood boxes and even miniature figures of the 'terracotta warriors'. None of these delights costs more than a few pounds, and some are only a few pence, yet buying them means more than acquiring a pleasing trinket, for the real appeal lies in entering the exotic world of the Orient—an art and culture that is enticingly different from our own.

These trinkets do not represent the real and ancient art and culture of China—rather, they are commercially produced for export. Nevertheless, you will also find earthenware pots and marble statues that are made in just the same way and to the same design as they have been for centuries. So although new, they represent the genuine traditions of Chinese craft and decoration and indeed are still used in China today.

However, if you travel the short distance from Liberty to the Victoria and Albert Museum in South Kensington, you can see some of the fine art of China's ancient civilization. The Far Eastern department has on display a large and impressive collection of painted screens, pottery, porcelain, furniture, sculpture and other *objets d'art* spanning many centuries. It is impossible not to be impressed and even overawed at the beauty of such work and the skill of those who sought to express through it the underlying discipline and the philosophy of their times, and the character of their natural surroundings.

Europe has had a long love affair with things Chinese, and the United States has a considerable Chinese community and hence cultural influence; the experience of London is repeated through many large stores and many museums throughout the Western world. Yet, in spite of the popular appeal of the idea of Chinese arts, their true quality and nature seem to have been hardly understood until the late nineteenth and early twentieth centuries. The arts of China were introduced to Europe by the Jesuits from about 1600, when a number of priests went to settle and work in the Far East. But in common with our attitude in those times to all new and 'different' cultures, Europe seems to have regarded Chinese arts as attractive and appealing, but somehow rather inferior. Instead of recognizing an ancient culture and philosophy of genius, from which the West might have something to learn or find some way of expanding its own realms of thought, the reaction was rather patronizing and arrogant, the image of the Far East one of exotic quaintness.

Europeans did not take the trouble to understand what Farrer called 'the commanding of the soul of the original' and instead perpetuated an over-simplified view as though this were the true

3 Courtyard garden at Hei Long
Tan (Black Dragon Pool)
Kunming, framed by moongate
with peach blossom decoration

4 Ornate window at Suzhou—
inspired by a spider's web
perhaps?

The valley noon:
one can hear no bell,
But wild bamboos
cut across bright clouds,
Flying cascades
hang from jasper peaks;

No one here knows
which way you have gone.

On visiting a Taoist Master in the Tai-
T'ien Mountains and Not Finding Him

style. The result was the development of the style of 'chinoiserie'. This pretty, domestic style is epitomized by the willow-pattern plate and echoed in the design of garden furniture and pavilions. It became phenomenally popular in the seventeen and eighteen hundreds, fuelled by the trading activities of the East Indies Companies. It was attractive and appealing as domestic design, but chinoiserie could not pretend to be fine art, nor to be truly representative of Chinese art and for these reasons it is understandably scorned by fine art scholars.

However, the twentieth century has seen a massive enlightenment among those nations which once considered their own culture, religion and philosophy to be naturally right and superior to all others. As we have learned more about life and people on other continents, so we have come to realize the foolishness of a closed mind and dogmatic attitude.

By the early 1900s the image of China was changing, as people had come to see the real art and something of the real character of the country. However, the most dramatic change from past attitudes has surely taken place in the last few years.

When our generation grew up, China was a closed and mysterious country. Our image of China was sketchy and confused; we seemed to hear much of its politics but little of its culture or the everyday life of its people—those things with which we could identify and which we might be able to understand by measuring against them the familiar pattern of our own lives.

The curiosity of our generation has been rewarded with the excitement of seeing China open up again. Unburdened by the artistic prejudices of the past, we are free to enjoy many varied images of China—its history, its art, its buildings, its landscape, its craft and its gardens. On a different level, perhaps the art scholars will forgive us for enjoying also the visual tradition of chinoiserie, for now that we no longer imagine it to be real Chinese art and that quaint, exotic image of China has been overtaken by newer, more powerful and truthful insights, we can appreciate its attractions at simple face value and just admire its everyday good looks.

5 Art imitates nature ...
ornamental ceramic 'bamboo
stems' at Qingympu Garden,
Nanchuang

The rich blue and white of willow patterned china, its impressive decorative design and pictures that tell a story; large, ornate vases and plates decorated with birds, butterflies and exotic flowers—full-blown pink peonies, golden chrysanthemums and creamy magnolias. The theme of Oriental flowers, birds and leaves has inspired many fabric designs that have become classics—as popular now as in Victorian times and beyond. The 'Chinese Chippendale' style of furniture and its many copies also continue to appeal and for the garden it is possible to buy a handsome new wooden seat based on a design by Lutyens, itself based on an original Chinese style.

We believe that there is now also room to take the many recently discovered images of China and allow them to inspire the art and craft of the West in a new way. It may seem pretentious to describe a garden as an art form, but the design of a garden is certainly a domestic art and its creation a practical craft; having created gardens with an Oriental feel or a hint of the exotic, we felt that the time was right to try to make a garden that might demonstrate an English-Chinese style, inspired by the images of China—and even of chinoiserie—as we now see them in the West.

Our garden designs have often included features that must have been almost unconsciously inspired by the Oriental approach—shingle and gravel for ground texture, plants placed individually so that their unusual or even misshapen outline could be appreciated; plants displayed sparingly in containers (often decorated Chinese containers); rocks and pebbles used as decoration because they are objects of beauty in their own right. This approach was already our common practice before we were aware of any particular source of inspiration.

For us, gardens are inspired not only by other gardens but by other fields of craftsmanship, from objects and landscapes that may seem quite unconnected.

Some garden designers see the introduction of stonework as a necessary evil, preferring to allow prominence always to flowers, but we see stonework as a potentially beautiful part of a garden and are fascinated by the use of stone and brick in buildings of all sorts. Where China is concerned, the Great Wall springs immediately to mind. Its sense of solidity and power are awesome, its very existence a feat that can only be wondered at. Although much of the wall is now crumbling, the restored section north of Peking portrays a clear picture of the stone and brick construction. The crenellated profile of the wall and its towers is impressive but not unfamiliar; more visually striking is the way in which its snaking course dips and rises, twists and turns in a beautiful progress through the land. The Tang dynasty lasted from about AD 600 to 900 in China and although at that time the wall was left to crumble and ruin as it may, this very decay was seen as a symbol of the fleeting nature of man's existence and the insignificance of his achievements.

The snaking course of the wall seems to find an echo in a feature that is sometimes seen in Chinese courtyards and gardens—a cloud wall, which has a flowing profile of regular curved scallops symbolic of passing clouds. Indeed, walls of

Seven horses; a wall plaque carved in marble.

enclosure are a very significant aspect of traditional Chinese architecture, for whole cities and towns were surrounded by them as well as individual temples, palaces and houses. A house would often be inside a walled courtyard and from the outside there was little to relieve the plainness other than a single pair of gates or a doorway. However the doors and roof were often decorated with fierce dragons, grotesque heads and figures of birds and animals. Their purpose was to act as guardians against evil spirits, but to the Western eye they are interesting as a form of decoration—especially as some of these figures, formed into ridge tiles, are now being imported into Britain. They are made of clay with a rich golden yellow glaze—a colour distinctive to the roof guardians found in the Imperial Palace in Peking, commonly known as the 'Forbidden City'. The beasts to be seen on the roofs there include such curiosities as a cockerel with a human figure riding on its back.

Some roofs have sweeping, upturned corners and this shape, too, is distinctive and memorable. Of course, the architecture of ordinary houses was nothing like as elaborate of that of palaces, temples and even garden pavilions. Nevertheless, one's eye is inevitably drawn to the most ornate and elaborate decoration—and hence to bright red columns supporting ceilings intricately painted to dazzling effect in green, red and gold. In China, red is a colour apparently associated with the south and with happiness and it is often used to ward off evil or ill fortune. That, we find, makes the visual appeal of red even stronger and its contrast with black all the more powerful, for black symbolized the north and water.

The shape of doorways, gates and arches is endlessly fascinating. They were built in abundance, since not only houses but complete cities were enclosed by walls and the gateways afforded a secure defence as well as symbolizing a well arranged and ordered society, according to the ancient rules and traditions. This notion is reported to be scorned in modern China as a hindrance to progress, but many varied gateways seem to remain and their shape, construction and decoration is often very beautiful. They range from plain, stark stone to those with carved pillars and colourfully tiled roofs or highly ornate wall tiles above graceful arches. Both the shape and decoration of gates and doorways and the added interest of their significance in society produce a compelling image that remains in the mind and sows the seed for new ideas.

Something of the shape and beauty of gateways is echoed in the varied and often highly elegant bridges of China. The idea of a passage across water appeals, as does the prospect of leaning over to gaze at rippling currents or still, quiet reflections. Chinese bridges are charming, not only for their practical purpose, but for their beautiful shape and decoration, especially those which form graceful arches or take a zig-zag course, as they often do in gardens.

It is not only Chinese architecture that captures the imagination of the West. Although we have already mentioned them as seeming to symbolize a new awareness of the country, the terracotta warriors cannot be ignored as a work of sculptural genius. The warriors were discovered in the tomb of Shihuang-Di, the first Emperor of China, who ruled during the Qin Dynasty 221–206 BC. He was responsible for forging the warring states of the previous Zhou Dynasty into one nation and for the construction of the Great Wall, as well as for the creation of a remarkable tomb complex at Xian. Here he planned to live on for ever, protected by the massive army modelled in terracotta.   The Great Wall.

6 An armoured warrior from the
museum for terracotta warriors
and horses near Shihuang-Di's
Tomb.

7 An armoured warrior.

8 A corner of the vast
museum of terracotta figures.

A highly decorative gateway.

The tomb is estimated to contain more than 8000 life-size warriors, horses and chariots—clay replicas of humans that would serve as substitutes for human sacrifice, providing the spirits of the dead with all the material needs of a life after death that was imagined to be similar to the world of the living.

Each figure was hand-modelled, the hollow arms and torso being formed from coils of wet grey clay and then mounted on to solid cylindrical legs. Details of clothing and armour were either worked on to the surface while it was still malleable, or separately shaped and added.

Superbly detailed heads lend the warriors an air of strength and individuality magnified by their size, for most are over six feet tall, and some are accompanied by horses.

The thriving tourist industry that now surrounds the tombs at Xian has led to the Chinese making contemporary reproductions of some of these warriors, ranging in size from a few inches to the massive equivalent of the original. One's mind goes back to Reginald Farrer's description of the oriental way of copying, for the modern reproductions are being made by the same method as the originals, and craftsmen are working through the same creative procedure as their ancient counterparts. Presumably they are rediscovering the experience of developing the particular skills and techniques that they would have employed.

Images of China would not be complete without the finely crafted and painted sculptured objects, pottery and porcelain. We think of jade, ivory, bronze, gold, silver as well as lacquered works and cloisonné. One can hardly fail to be inspired by the lingering images, not only of beautiful, satisfying, exotic shapes but also of infinite, perfect details, of filigree lines and minute,

Flying chestnut champs long reins,
Winging, winging turns the light wheels.
My lover looks down as he fords green flowing torrents,
Looks up as he crosses the hill's nine folds.
The long path is winding and perilous,
Autumn plants grow on both sides.

Yellow blossoms like heaps of gold,
White flowers like scattered silver,
Green buds shoot kingfisher tints,
Crimson corollas image red clouds.

And in their midst dew-laden boughs,
Purple blossoms enshrining plain scent
Hang luxurious in patterns crystalline,
Wafting fragrance and freshness.

My eyes grow dizzy with glorious designs,
My mind whirls with wondrous colours.
I soothe my heart, mourn the lone traveller,
Look down and up, feel self-pity.
I pause with a sigh by the garden wall,
Take my pen and compose this verse.

Crystalline

9 A porcelain jar painted in enamel
colours dating from the early
sixteenth century

10 Stone bridge at the Summer
Palace, Beijing, has an elegant
shape and striking stonework detail and decoration

close patterns. Remarkable, too, is the continuity of design that has been perpetuated through thousands of years, for China has the world's largest unbroken cultural history—and much of this must be due to the tradition of 'copying' from previous masters of the particular art or craft that was being learned, of understanding the 'commanding soul of the original' and eventually translating them into 'more or less new form, in terms of one's own taste and time'.

This is certainly true of painting and calligraphy, and must have applied to the forms of decoration of silk—the material that is inextricably linked with China and the basis of so much trade. Here, one really does enter the realms of fine art and our purpose is not to trace its history and philosophy—which would demand a scholarly expertise and a good deal of space—but to reflect on the overwhelming impression that remains in the mind.

This must surely be one of the recurrent themes of the natural world, for so often the subject of a painting is rocks or mountains, lakes, birds, butterflies, trees or flowers. This reflects a traditional philosophy of China whose understanding is not merely the domain of specialist scholars and experts—it is so fundamental that anyone who takes even a passing interest in the Chinese way of life and of thought is likely to encounter the idea. Quite simply, it is the interdependence of man with the natural world and the absolute need for an orderly existence which is in harmony with nature. There was of course a practical basis for this belief in a country whose economy was based on agriculture, but it is manifest in a spiritual way in the themes of visual art and of poetry.

Of course, one cannot tell how much of the original is lost in the English translations available, but dipping into the poetry of several centuries it is possible to appreciate enough to be moved by the passion of the expression of love and longing. Longing for the return of a lover is often associated with watching the blossom of peach or plum blow gently in the wind or float slowly downstream. Trees are invoked—perhaps covered in frost—snow-clad mountains and of course the cool, white light of the moon. The setting for the poem is often a view of a garden ...

Dragon roof decoration.

In front of K'ung-ming Shrine
stands an old cypress,
With branches like green bronze
and roots like granite;

Its hoary bark, far round,
glistens with raindrops,
and blueblack hues, high up,
blend in with Heaven's:

Long ago Statesman, King
kept Time's appointment,
But still this standing tree
has men's devotion;

Wide, wide though writhing roots,
maintain its station,
Far, far in lonely heights,
many's the tempest

When its hold is the strength
of Divine Wisdom
and straightness by the work
of the Creator....

The Ballad of The Ancient Cypress

11 The Great Wall.

13 A bright blue glazed animal from the eaves of a hall in the garden of Emperor Qianlong.

12 A section of the Beijing grand view garden used in the film *A Dream of Red Mansions.*

The white dagoba at the
Miaoying Buddhist Monastery in
Beijing.

Chinoiserie porcelain designs.

14 Tables and stools with azaleas
in pots and arrangements of rock
in the Garden of the Humble
Administrator, Suzhou

Let the South Wind blow you back my heart,
Fly and land it in the Tavern court
Where, to the East, there are sprays and leaves
of one peach-tree, sweeping the blue mist;

This is the tree I myself put in
When I left you, nearly three years past;
A peach-tree now, level with the eaves,
And I sailing cannot yet turn home!

Pretty daughter, P'ing-yang is your name,
Breaking blossom, there beside my tree,
Breaking blossom you cannot see me
And your tears flow like the running stream.

Letter To His Two Small Children
Staying In Eastern Lu At Wen Yang
Village Under Turtle Mountain

Sunlight begins to fade,
mist fills the flowers,
The moon as white as silk
weeps and cannot sleep,

This song has a meaning
that no one can tell,
It follows the Spring wind
as far as Yen-jan

To you far, far away
beyond the blue sky—

If you do not believe
that my heart breaks,
Come back and look with me
into this glass!

Longing

My south neighbour has a fine tree,
It greets the sun, stretches white blooms,
Sleek fronds sheathe long boughs,

Green leaves screen red stems.
With the wind it breathes faint whispers,
Perfumed air pierces purple mist.

My heart burns for this tree,
I long to move it near my home.
At dusk, I would stroll underneath,
At dawn caress its corollas.

How deep and firm the roots!
So mean and low my home!
To transplant it is a hopeless dream,
The sighs I sigh, what good are they?

Fine Tree

15 Circular moongate frames
a bamboo vista in a garden at
Wuyon Hill, Leshan

'A perpetual renewal of life'

EUROPE AND AMERICA owe many familiar and favourite garden plants to intrepid plant hunting expeditions to China undertaken during the nineteenth and early twentieth centuries. Soon after the country was opened up again, the hunting trips resumed and continue today, adding to our knowledge and the range of plants available that may have started their life on the lower slopes of some remote Chinese mountain, although never cultivated at all in Chinese gardens.

It took a little longer to start to familiarize ourselves with the gardens of China and the process continues today. It seems that we still have a long way to go before we really understand, although many people have been introduced to the fact that a distinctive Chinese style exists by the excellent book, *The Chinese Garden* by Maggie Keswick. In Britain, there is still a good deal of confusion between Chinese and Japanese and there are people who, like some art scholars at the turn of the century, can see no difference between the two styles. Others have tried to copy slavishly, without really understanding what they see (we return once again to Farrer's complaint) but even in the seventeenth century the British were trying to learn.

At that time the Western garden was influenced by neo-classicism, where beauty was deemed to lie in formal symmetry and regular straight lines. Sir William Temple was a garden enthusiast who in 1683 wrote an essay in which he compared the British style with that of the Chinese:

> 'Among us, the beauty of building and planting is placed chiefly in some certain proportions, symmetries, or uniformities; our walks and our trees ranged so as to answer one another, and at exact distances. The Chinese scorn this way of planting, and say, a boy that can tell a hundred, may plant walks of trees in straight lines, and over-against one another, and to what length and extent he pleases. But their greatest reach of imagination is employed in contriving figures, where the beauty shall be great, and strike the eye, but without any order or disposition of parts that shall be commonly observed.'

In his observation of the great difference between the Chinese and European styles, Sir William was undoubtedly perceptive, but it is impossible to accept his theory that because the Chinese style appears more natural, it is not subject to any rules or order. Another commentator of the time defined this seeming disorder as really being 'rhythm in disguise', for nothing is haphazard; everything is subject to an underlying desire for an ordered harmony with nature which nonetheless expresses creativity and imagination.

Only the Chinese could create a genuine Chinese garden and it is an art that has almost disappeared today. All we can do is

The catkins line the lanes,
making white carpets,
And leaves on lotus streams
spread like green money:

Pheasants root bamboo shoots,
nobody looking,
While ducklings on the sands
sleep by their mothers.

Nine Short Songs:
Wandering Breezes: 8

16 Latticed gallery window at Liu Yuan—Lingering Garden—Suzhou

The autumn wind is light,
the autumn moon is bright;
Fallen leaves gather but then disperse,
a cold crow roosts but again he stirs;
I think of you and wonder when I'll see you again?
At such an hour, on such a night, cruel is love's pain!

Three, Five, Seven Words

Ornamental window designs.

19 Decorative window in a classical Chinese garden at Suzhou

17 Top left: Cloud wall at Yi Yuan—the Garden of Ease—in Suzhou

18 Left: Two latticed windows, each in a different geometric style, in the Lingering Garden, Suzhou

A wall plaque depicting two
serene heads.

observe, hope to understand, let the impressions become absorbed by our minds, senses and emotions and allow them to influence ideas for our own gardens where the original mood and philosophy is not replicated but provides a detectable underlying theme.

Western garden style is no longer rigid, formal and symmetrical, as it was when Sir William Temple wrote. Indeed, in gardens as in other forms of domestic art and craft, we have almost achieved a pinnacle of eclectic and catholic taste where just about anything goes—the expression of the individual is all and we are free to indulge in whatever style we please. Nevertheless, through the traditions of the herbaceous border and sweeping lawn of the ever popular English country house garden; through the assertive ideas of William Robinson and the more gentle, inspired touch of Gertrude Jekyll, we have become used to a natural approach, but one that is colourful and luxuriant. We must have softness, flowers, colour and interest all the year round.

Against this background a first glimpse of pictures of Chinese gardens is stark in the extreme. The overwhelming feature is not a host of tumbling plants, but a restrained, strange, mysterious relationship of rocks and water. Rock is used as an object of beauty, carefully positioned on its own or in a group with others, and prized for its shape and character. Plants are used only sparingly.

Of course, it would be foolish to pretend that all gardens in China look alike. As with any garden style, each design and each situation varies, possessing its own features and characteristics. However, it is the features and materials common to many that have inspired us and in looking at those, it is necessary to make what might appear to be sweeping generalizations.

Historically, whether they were Imperial pleasure grounds on a lavish scale or more modest undertakings by literary scholars or administrators working in cities, Chinese gardens reflected distinctive themes. The relationship between man and nature has always been important, and nature is intended to be reflected and symbolized in gardens—the mountains were thought of as the home of the Immortals; a simple pavilion amongst trees symbolizes the idea of a simple farmer's life in a cottage set in an orchard; spring blossom is to be appreciated not only for its own fragile beauty but also as a symbol of the growth and regeneration of spring and the seasonal work on the land.

Some gardens were built to reflect wealth and status, others as a setting for the enjoyment of literature, poetry and scholarly pursuits. In either case, the garden was a place not only for observation and contemplation; it was also a setting for active enjoyment and socializing and most certainly a place set apart from the everyday world—from the cares and burdens of working life and the daily round. This philosophy has held true in China since hundreds of years BC, and yet it is one with which any garden lover living in the Western world in the late twentieth century would surely identify and sympathize.

As already mentioned, Chinese houses were traditionally enclosed by walls, and the buildings within that enclosure were

20 Pots of primulas and
calceolarias arranged on an open
lattice window at Tanghua
Temple, Kunming

required to run along a particular axis and face a certain direction; everything was arranged in a symmetrical, orderly manner. Gardens, too, are enclosed by walls—sometimes as a completely separate space, sometimes within the courtyard area of the house complex—but their shape is not regular and symmetrical. Instead, they are planned to give a more random, organic feel that emphasizes their difference and separateness from the routine domestic surroundings. Within the garden, there are many architectural features, but the experience and shape are flowing and organic.

Not only is the outline of the layout apparently unstructured. Within the garden, it is never possible to see everything at once in some wide open vista. Rather, one secluded space leads to another, one feature to another; through illusion and mystery the visitor is led through a series of impressions. The immediate view will always present a complete picture and yet always seems to lead on to something equally tantalizing and surprising beyond. Each small picture may consist of a single rock with interesting shape, a tree in blossom, an arrangement of pots, a group of bamboo, and it will often be viewed through a moongate, a window or a lattice grille, which frames the vista and creates a sense of greater depth and perspective, greater illusion.

The individual vistas or 'pictures' are painted not only with obvious visual interest in mind. The viewer is certainly intended to see a whole series of decorative and pleasing images, but is also expected to appreciate a sense of symbolism and metaphor. Rocks symbolizing mountains; streams suggesting rivers and pools reminiscent of larger lakes. The metaphoric features may be as simple as the shape of a window or the decorative motif on top of a wall, and they seem to be created in a spirit of lightness and enjoyment. There does not seem to be the intention of challenging the onlooker to understand some weighty intellectual inference, but rather of delighting the spirit with a sense of pleasant surprise as a view is encountered and enjoyed and then the symbolism is appreciated. This sense of enjoyment and surprise in arrangement and decoration proved a powerful inspiration to us.

Part of the underlying philosophy of the garden is the concept of contrasts—of yang and yin—and here we return to the importance of man's harmony with nature. Yang and yin symbolize earth and heaven—the two great powers in nature which are complete opposites and must always be balanced and reconciled. Yin is dark, female and passive whilst yang is bright, male and active.

In gardens, these symbolic opposites create constant contrast. A solid wall is pierced by a light, decorative, open screen or window or a moon gate allows a tantalizing view beyond. Powerful, upright rugged rocks are set against deep, cool, reflective water and the natural form of plants contrasts with man-made paths and pavements, often with interesting textures and sometimes containing decorative figures formed from pebbles.

Of the elements that go to make up the Chinese garden, rock

Sculpted wall relief with ducks
and lotus blossom.

is probably the most important and the most prized. Mountains were seen in ancient tradition as the home of the Immortals, and in gardens rocks are deemed to symbolize the mountains. Chinese landscape painting shows mountains as craggy and rugged and so the most prized rocks for gardens became limestone that occurred naturally on the beds of lakes and had been worn by water over many years to an almost tortuous shape that for us has a mysterious, lunar quality. Rocks may be positioned separately or in groups and they can be very beautiful, although the more extreme shapes (those traditionally prized) are perhaps too strange to the Western eye and we find ourselves appreciating their weird character rather than their beauty. Nevertheless, water-worn rocks are a feature that is inextricably linked with the Chinese garden.

Just as rocks symbolize mountains, so water symbolizes a river or lake and is almost equally important. Water may feature in a single expanse or it may take the form of a meandering stream that opens out into a wider, informal pool or lake. Sometimes lotus blossom will float delicately across the water surface; sometimes the surface is nearly obscured by a density of green lotus pads. The water is often crossed by a bridge, or several interlinking bridges that form a zig-zag shape, creating interesting lines and a sense of illusion.

A pavilion—often with a highly decorative shape—may be positioned in the centre of lake, with access by means of a bridge. Evil spirits were believed to travel only in straight lines, and so the pavilion approached by a zig-zag bridge was seen as a place of goodness and happiness.

Walls serve to enclose spaces within the garden as well as the boundary itself, and yet one can peer through a lattice screen or window set in the wall to glimpse what lies ahead. The design of the screen or window can be quite elaborate and is always based on some theme of nature. So, too, do the shapes of moon gates vary, but they have a striking ability to frame a part of the view and create a living picture.

There is no lawn in a Chinese garden, nor anything like it. Ground surfaces are of stone or even rocks or compacted earth. Surfaces vary and are often decoratively textured. On paths and paved areas there may be mosaics made from coloured pebbles, usually depicting animals or birds.

Ground patterns are just as important as three-dimensional views and designs. Pebble and stone arrangements not only look decorative, but serve the purpose of defining the different areas of the garden, changing as the visitor walks from one part to another.

Plants are used more sparingly than in Western gardens and tend to be positioned individually or in small groups so that their form, outline and texture can be appreciated throughout the changing seasons. Textures are appreciated for their subtlety, and plant forms used to restrained effect. The overwhelming impression seems to be one of green with occasional splashes of colour and, not unnaturally, bamboo is used frequently, as are low, grassy hummocks set close to rocks. That is not to say that flowering plants are unimportant, for those flowers which we

21 Water-worn rock—prized for
its shape and texture

22 Water-carved rocks in the
Garden of the Fisherman, Suzhou

23 Arrangement of stones in a
vase; both form and texture are
beautiful in their own right and
displayed as such

Hydrangeas in a Chinese pot.

associate with the familiar images of Chinese paintings are often seen. Camellias, magnolias, roses, chrysanthemums and prunus are considered beautiful but historically the most sought after garden flower was the tree peony, its lush blooms much appreciated and admired in early summer. Indeed, summer was seen as the season for flowers and plants and no demands were made on them to perform throughout the year, as we are accustomed to do. Other seasons brought their own different interest and character to the garden, such as spring breezes, the autumn moon or winter snow.

A display of plants in pots seems to be a common sight in China, not only in gardens and courtyards but also in open public areas. In gardens a special bench or series of shelves might be made to accommodate them and a courtyard might contain what seems to be a whole garden grown in pots, including trees. Plants may be grown for their colourful flowers or for their architectural shapes—sometimes dwarfed or quite contorted. We have become familiar in the West with the Japanese style of bonsai, but the concept of dwarfed plants and trees grown in shallow pots originated in China, where it still flourishes and is known as penjing.

This brief look at some of the features of traditional Chinese gardens demonstrates that the approach is quite unfamiliar to Western ideas of gardening. Yet, even if the gardens of China seem stark and austere to those used to a more lush appearance with greater horticultural emphasis, the purpose behind their creation does bear some comparison, for both styles of garden share the aim to please and divert, to allow the visitor to enter a world that is in distinct contrast to life's everyday round of work and care, to contemplate quietly and admire the beauty all round, to enjoy a sense of harmony with the natural world, and even a feeling of spiritual well-being.

One can compare, too, the effect of the garden styles, for although very different in appearance, each has inspired a succession of poets, artists and writers, whether as the subject of their work or simply as a setting conducive to its creation. There was a tradition in ancient times for Chinese poets and calligraphers to have a pavilion or a room of the house which overlooked the garden, emphasizing again the theme of striving to be at peace with nature. Nowadays, the traditional gardens of China are open as popular tourist attractions just like the gardens of famous British country estates, so they are enjoyed and wondered at in a different way and by a whole new generation, symbolizing perhaps the perpetual renewal of life.

24 Dramatic bamboo stems at the Hangzou Botanical Garden

25 Ornamental bamboo at the Canton Botanic Garden

The tall terrace stirs with spring's flush,
Clear pools reflect sunlit splendour,
Green mallow twists toward sunlight,
Kingfisher willow slants with the wind.
In the woods a bird startles my heart,
Orchard's massed blooms captivate my eyes.
Like me they all know this season,
Sigh that you alone keep far from home.
The traveller will not come back today,
Why bother to pick a vain hempen pledge?

Spring Sun

26 Pebble mosaic depicting a pair
of deer

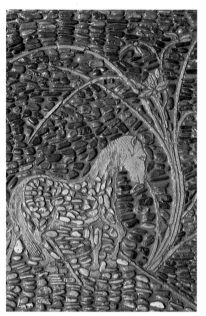

27 Pebble mosaic of horse with
plant incorporates flowing,
swirling lines

28 Goldfish pebble mosaic in
garden path demonstrates the
Chinese fondness for highly
ornately bred creatures

Before my bed
There is bright moonlight
So that it seems
Like frost on the ground:

Lifting my head
I watch the bright moon,
Lowering my head
I dream that I'm home.

Quiet Night Thoughts

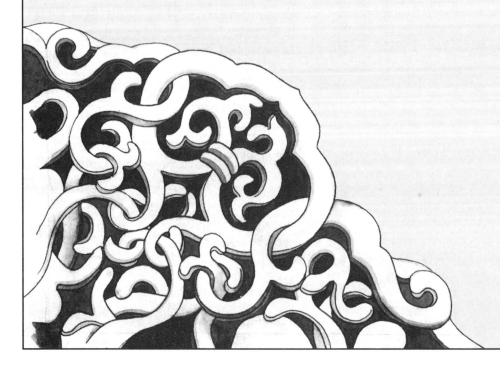

Peach and plum I put in
were not ownerless:
The old boy's wall, though low,
does mark a garden:

So like the winds of Spring
by stealth to rob them,
At night to come and blow
and break some blossom!

Nine Short Songs:
Wandering Breezes: 3

CHINESE-INSPIRED GARDEN STYLE

29 The bridge design is simple but elegant, displaying both strength and a sense of movement. The board surface is decorated by variegated ivies in pots

'More or less new form, in terms of one's own taste and time'

TO THE WEST, China—its art and history—has revealed itself as never before. Some enigma still remains however—a distinct sense of strangeness, of difference and mystery which is part of the appeal of the very idea of the country. We wanted to try to create something inspired by that enigma before it is lost. Hopefully that will never happen, but in this age of global tourism there may be a danger that for many people China becomes a series of images of tourist spots, aeroplanes and international hotels that hardly distinguish it from other countries.

Intending to make a garden, we did not see why we should restrict our thoughts to the *gardens* of China. The authentic Chinese style seems, after all, very stark. Western taste is for a more luxuriant look and so we tried to accommodate this by introducing other images of China not normally found in a garden. We were intrigued by all forms of the country's arts and crafts and by the poignant images left in the mind by the Queen's visit—perhaps the epitome of West meeting East.

We took images of many aspects of Chinese art, architecture and culture and expressed them in the form of a garden. Inevitably, the images of China are distilled. The garden is seen as theatre. Looking through a small grille and peering at the framed view beyond is like seeing a miniature dramatic production. The constant aim of Chinese gardens to take the visitor through a series of new vistas and moods reminds one in some way of making progress through a staged exhibition.

Increasingly, pots, statues and other items made in China to traditional designs are coming into Europe and America and being marketed for use in gardens. Some would never be seen in a garden, but in some other setting in China, and yet they will find their way into Western gardens—and why not? The only exception might be if they occurred in a ridiculous way—perhaps a white marble Buddha as the centrepiece of a suburban lawn. It seems the right time to suggest some ideas as to how these items could be placed in a setting that captures an appropriate mood and style, hopefully avoiding the ridiculous. The Chinese are keen to export, to promote trade—and with an exchange of trade, after all, comes an exchange of ideas and styles.

In China, some of the traditional gardens created for palaces and the houses of wealthy men were—not surprisingly—quite large. They were not the common domain of ordinary people who needed to use the land available to them to grow food and keep livestock. But our particular interest has often been in creating gardens on a scale that means something to an ordinary householder. Of course, there is great satisfaction in transforming a large site—but the more so if it is for the enjoyment of

A pair of hand-carved stone
horses with riders.

30 A striking form of sculpture
set amongst plants and an
unmistakable image of China:
a lifesize replica of a terracotta
warrior made in China and
transported to London for the
Chinese Puzzle Garden

31 Image of China: the bridge
leads to ponds overlooked by
white marble geese, whilst a
carefully sculpted arrangement of
rock with bamboo create a
'miniature landscape'. The small,
half-hidden figure of a warrior is
echoed by its larger counterpart

Buddha with pebbles and plants.

many, rather than one person or a small family. This feeling is not prompted by political belief or social philosophy; it is just a personal reaction based on the desire to communicate new ideas to as large and receptive an audience as possible.

Communicating ideas to those interested in gardens is one of the purposes of the gardens at London's Chelsea Show which is, after all, one of the world's most prestigious horiticultural events. It was there that we chose to follow through some of the inspirations and feelings that had been lingering in the back of our minds, filling our own garden with plants in earthenware pots covered in images of dragons, birds, butterflies, bamboo, lakes and mountains, and placing pebbles beside them just because they are beautiful.

It seems to us that people are ready for a more adventurous style in their gardens. Of course, they want a garden that is not too demanding to maintain and which can be used as a focal point for social life as the living room can, but perhaps they want something offering escape, a chance to experience a new and different approach to a familiar setting. We are now a highly sophisticated society—the old ways won't do. It is not enough to fill a garden with plants; there must be a structural framework that presents interesting moods and vistas all year round. We can appreciate something more sophisticated, too, than the old fruit salad colours of the mixed shrub border burgeoning with rhododendrons. The colour schemes of Gertrude Jekyll have made a big comeback—people appreciate the subtlety of thought and experimentation behind her work—the effort required to achieve such apparently artless creativity. Colour schemes are appreciated rather than a riot of colour, and the themes behind the visible finish—the story of what went into that which we see before us—are seized with fascination.

Perhaps that more adventurous style will embrace something of the Oriental. In the United States there is already a strong tradition of Japanese gardens, both authentic and Western inspired. Perhaps Chinese gardens, too, are growing in popularity. Europe may be less cosmopolitan, but here too we seem ready to become inspired to new things by the traditions of Oriental style, adapting them to be comfortable to our taste. But not so comfortable that they lose all sense of excitement....

If you have a theme, you have to have a name, and we called our Chelsea Show garden the Chinese Puzzle Garden. Why? Because it might be a puzzle to anyone who expected an authentic Chinese garden? Certainly we were told by one assertive person 'I've been to China and I've never seen anything like *this*', but she came back to have a second look.... Because people would assume that the puzzle had an answer and start to look for it? Well, some did, so they had to take a good hard look.... Because the shape of the design was reminiscent of the pieces of a Chinese puzzle that may or may not fit together—one for which there is no real solution? And because the zig-zag effect of the shapes reminded one of the zig-zag bridges that span rock and water as the mysteries of the Chinese garden unfold? The puzzle may be all of those things. Oriental is inscrutable.

32 A chair ... or is it sculpture? Black wood and natural wood, straight lines and curves—the contrast of yin and yang, with echoes of calligraphy in the art of the simple back rest

33 Planters for a Western garden inspired by Chinese urn stands echo the dramatic theme of red and black

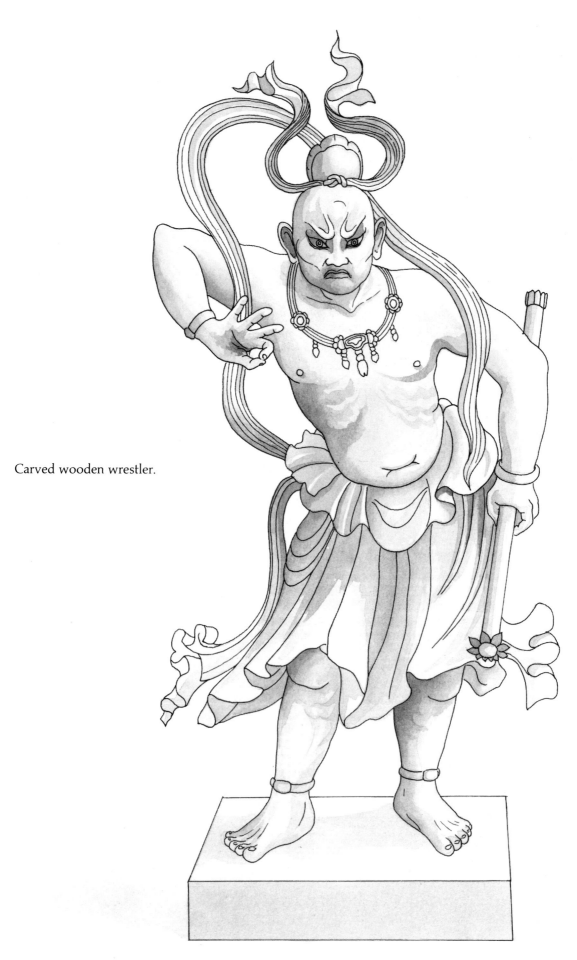

Carved wooden wrestler.

The design is for quite a small garden, but it could go on further—the hint is there. Beyond the wall or the dragon screen might lie some different view, another part of the garden with another mood or change of character. Although small, the garden must not look overcrowded; the onlooker should have the impression of a number of interesting features, of parts of the whole that possess their own identity, and should appreciate those with space between. Only then should the realization dawn that all those highpoints of attention are actually contained within a space that seems deceptively large, but is in fact quite small. That is the principle by which we have worked for a long time and that is the major philosophy of the Chinese garden—only there it is taken more literally, for like the gradual unrolling of a Chinese scroll, where the whole must never be visible but each piece slowly revealed and then concealed again, the different areas of a Chinese garden only come into view as one moves from one point to another.

The design is set on an axis—a forty-five degree angle to what would be the house, and to the first window through which it would be viewed. The irregular shape of the boundary indeed indicates that in another, larger space something more would lie beyond the eye.... This may not be the end, but only the beginning.

Illusion is attempted; only the onlooker can judge whether it has been achieved. The channels of water might seem to suggest that if you tried for long enough the pieces could fit together, might comfortably interlock to solve the puzzle. But that would be an ending, and all hope of mystery would be spoiled.

Shapes are important, and—in accordance with the Chinese principles of yin and yang—they should be balanced. This means a balance of horizontal and vertical lines; levels vary slightly, the bridge giving horizontal emphasis but tall stems of bamboo creating strong vertical lines. Flat space is broken up by high points—especially with plants and sometimes with pots—and is framed by vertical walls and screens. The bridge and the channels of water emphasize the straight lines, but they are balanced by a circular design on the paving and groups of round pots. Circles and straight lines; harsh shapes and blurred softness; upright and flat.

Red is for happiness and the south; black is for water and the north. That, we understand, is their intriguing meaning in China. To Western eyes, the two colours can readily combine to conjure images simply of China itself. We have seen pavilions, furniture, fabrics, dishes and trays with huge splashes or tiny hints of these colours, and they work equally well in a garden. The colour scheme is a means of stating the Oriental theme and of adding brightness and luxuriance against a quiet background. The light in Britain is so often dull, but why always play safe? Perhaps black and red are a surprise, but when lifted by the soft greens and yellows of plants they are not hard to live with.

Bright colour can have an uplifting effect. When too many colours combine, the effect is jarring and unsatisfying, but when a scheme is detectable, the onlooker can apppreciate not only the colour itself but can share the idea behind it. Red busy lizzies

34 Square blue-glazed
earthenware pot is beautiful in
itself; simply planted with
Ageratum it is complemented by
a backdrop of 'tumbling' plants
and pebbles

35 Plants with a harmonizing
theme of yellow, green and red,
the red tips of Photinia stems
echoing the red dragon motif in
the background

Conifer in a decorated
earthenware pot.

Into my bedcurtains drift fireflies,
In front of the garden purple orchids bloom.
Nature withers, sensing the change of season,
Swans arrive telling of travellers cold.
Your journey may end at winter's close,
I'll wait till late spring for your return.

Poem Sent to a Traveller

Buddha set amongst boulders and
planted pots.

36 Reflections in water …
floating pebbles … marble geese
and carved red dragons …
reflections of the garden as
theatre

37 Not Chinese in origin, but something of the Chinese tradition in the way these plants are chosen and arranged to display their shape, form and colour

match exactly the red of the timberwork highlights; the contrast of silver foliage and black stain; the hint of deep blue in the flowers of the Blue Mountain Lupin which echo the 'chun'—meaning 'sky after rain'—glaze of Chinese earthenware pots. The tips of photinia leaves are red; the stems of camellias are crimson and *Acer palmatum* 'Atropurpureum' introduces deep, musty, purply shades lifted by clear white and hints of soft mauve primulas in pots. Yin and yang. The contrast of dark with light and bright.

Black contrasts with the red brickwork of walls—mature stock bricks with subtle metallic shading worthy of being enjoyed for their own character as well as a steady foil for soft green bamboo swaying, rustling, shivering, whispering. Bright red lifts the buffness and greyness of weathered shaded paving. All these tones seem to settle comfortably of their own accord and harmonize in an almost surprising way with the earthy golden and green shades of glazed, decorated earthenware and golden foliage tints.

Colour is a feature of stone and rock, but texture is equally strong. Corinium paving is like circular mosaics of stone with slightly rugged relief. It has a mellow, age-old look that seems to echo the paths and paved areas of Chinese gardens, the deliberately decorative texture of pebble arrangements if not their visual images. Loose stone chippings bring a texture of relief to the ground. Plants grow through them and they take on a pleasing irregular softness.

Chippings are irregular slivers of a once solid mass, now edged and angled, but round, smooth pebbles are satisfyingly complete. This perfection is pleasing to handle and to arrange in mounds and drifts to decorate, to contrast squareness and angles, to add balance to a composition of plants or pots. Clean grey and subtle pink; smooth pebbles may not have the excitement of water-worn rock—their role is to please in a quieter way. Their arrangement appears to have happened artlessly—perhaps theatrically, as art sets out to imitate life and convince its audience that this indeed is life itself. . . .

Contrast in texture. Yin and yang. Rugged stone with smooth glazed earthenware; with water; with fragile looking, slender bamboo stems. Downy silvery leaves with the leathery gloss of camellias and rhododendrons; soft black wood that is warm to the touch, and the coolness of white birds sculpted from solid marble.

Rock is essential to Chinese gardens—rock arranged for its own impressive shape, again the contrast of tall, dramatic outlines with low, half-buried, bulky shapes that seem to hug the ground more safely. Water-worn limestone from China does not exist in Britain, so native rock is subject to the skilled hand and eye, the sure touch of a sculptor who understands stone and loves it for its own sake.

Pieces of rock are rolled and levered into position to create balanced arrangements. One is based around one tall and two lower shapes representing the host and his two guests—a traditional Chinese theme. When positions are considered right, both as groups and as balanced focal points of the design, the

Yu-lin stone lions.

38 Screen, planting and large
pebbles form shapes that descend
in a flowing line to ground level,
where water gives depth of
reflection.

39 A vista across the Chinese
Puzzle Garden—Chinese style
translated into a Western garden

more delicate task of the sculptor's tools begins to work its magic. Gradually, two pieces are merged into one large whole; the surface begins to change character, slowly chipped and carved to echo the weird fascination of the Chinese original which has taken a long time of observation and consideration to produce the results of a day. As the dust is washed away, a translation of the original source of inspiration is revealed.

In Chinese gardens rocks are admired for their own sculptural quality. Sculpture in the form of the images of creatures, human beings, the Buddha are traditionally associated with tombs or temples. But now China is producing these figures for Western consumption. Copies are being made of the magnificent terracotta warriors by the same method as in 210 BC for twentieth-century Europe. Especially to meet the demands of other countries, Tianjin Stone and Wood Carvings are created in Herbei Province, Northern China. Famous ancient works are reproduced here, made painstakingly by skilled and careful hands.

Do we offend Chinese sensibilities by using these figures for garden decoration? Not at all, for that is part of their purpose, as the compelling introduction to the illustrated brochure describes:

> 'Some other items handled by this corporation are suitable for the decoration and construction of pavilions and terraces, bridges and gardens, such as grand lions, awe-inspiring unicorns, strong and vigorous Tang horses, fat and lovely ducks. Perfect finishing through a pure hand-made process from material selection to carving, polish and antique finish, all of the products are done with minute carving, fluent lines, correct proportion and lifelike images.'

Hence two fairly fat but certainly lovely and elegant geese grace the edge of a water channel.

Other decoration includes a beautifully sculptured sinewy figure of a writhing dragon—a hint of mystery and intrigue stretched along the top of a wall, its rearing head a delightful sight that can be glimpsed almost accidentally.

Dragons were traditionally the decorative symbol which signified the Emperor; the Forbidden City is rich with such images. We took the design of a small jade buckle made two thousand years ago and skilled carpentry created dragon motifs to grace the panels of the dramatic black zig-zag screen—a highlight of bright red across the view of the garden.

Marble statue of a Buddha.

40 An interpretation of the
Oriental style with a modern feel
by Steve Prescott (Telegraph
Garden, Chelsea Show)

41 In a corner of the same garden a carved wooden sculpture is centrepiece of a quiet composition with brickwork and planting

Wall frieze.

Imaginative design and skilful carpentry by woodworking students enable the garden to feature new, original timberwork that, like the design of the garden itself, is inspired by traditional images of China. The bridge has clean horizontal lines and—in keeping with much Oriental woodwork, whether for architectural or smaller-scale use—the design deliberately makes a pleasing feature of joints, and methods of construction are visible. They are as much a part of the overall effect as the clean lines and details of shaping, with hints of upturned and chamfered ends.

The design of the table similarly makes a feature of its means of construction, while the elegant small chair is unusually decorative in shape—almost sculptural in its own right. This effect is emphasized by the design of the chair back with cleverly interwoven pieces of wood that appear to have been bent like metal to create shapes reminiscent of a Chinese character. Suddenly an image, a memory springs to mind of the childhood game of Chinese Chequers. Mysterious lines and figures around the edge; we all try to decipher them but the enigma remains. . . .

Earthenware pots are from China itself, made to the designs that have pleased for centuries in Jiangsu Province. Wooden planters are newly designed and made, but they seem just as appropriate, their shape and style reminiscent of elegant indoor stands and furniture designs that one might see in an Imperial Palace—or even the Victoria and Albert Museum.

A planter might display colourful flowers or a strangely shaped pine in the style of penjing; its tall base could also form a stand for a sculpture or a piece of rock that appeals for its sculptural quality.

The sculptural focal point—probably the first life-size reproduction of a terracotta soldier from the tomb of Shihuang-Di to be brought into Britain. To many, the greyness of the terracotta in that part of China is quite a surprise, but the greatest impression for which one cannot be prepared—in spite of weeks of anticipation before its actual arrival—is the sheer sense of power and presence of this vast, solid, heavy figure with its noble mien and formal stance. The face is awesome, the uniform detail somehow intricate, the knowledge that its original counterpart was made over two thousand years ago quite overwhelming and very hard to comprehend, for our historic scale of measurement has rarely had to come to terms with quite such dramatic reality. The product of an ancient, warlike civilization in a twentieth century London park. . . .

A much smaller warrior figure is glimpsed like an echo—an illusion of perspective perhaps which creates its own theatrical scene with rocks and bamboo. A Chinese landscape in miniature? The impression of a complete scene, an area with its own mood and character that might be viewed through a decorative grille and slowly unfold. Here it is more clearly visible and suggests ideas to the Western eye, for others like this small warrior are starting to find their way into gardens and this, maybe, is one idea for sympathetic display.

In China it is considered entirely appropriate and even symbolic to contrast the rugged character and permanence of rock—perhaps even the sense of history that pervades our

42 Breezewood Garden,
Maryland, USA. An American
interpretation of Chinese style
with a striking arrangement of
rocks against a background of the
strong vertical lines of tall trees

A straight tree growing by a river
Fell ill, so became a thing of beauty.
At dawn from cloudy hair it parts,
At night to moth eyebrows draws close.

The Gnarled Pillow

warrior sculpture—with the more fragile appearance and ephemeral nature of plants.

Although the garden has an exotic feel, many of the plants that feature are far from rare and not all are those that would necessarily be found in a Chinese garden. Again, the important principle is to capture the look and character of the original—to allow its influence to work but to combine that with planting which is softer, more abundant than the very stark feel which seems so alien to Western eyes.

Shrubs—in strategically positioned groups or in pots—make a framework. Specimens of evergreen photinia with its reddish stems and red-tipped leaves; camellias that will bloom in soft, blousy fullness; rhododendrons; the lovely leaf form of pieris; spreading bushy pines; *Acer palmatum* with its finely formed leaves and light, spreading stems—specimens whose shape deserves to be appreciated and admired as they stand almost alone and uncluttered. Tall, slender bamboo, the essential Chinese plant.

Plant form and foliage colour are essential—sword-like phormiums and *Astelia* 'Silver Spear'; lush broad-leaves hostas; trailing ivies variegated gold or splashed with grey and white.

Flower colour is achieved by using humble, familiar plants in a different way. White sweet alyssum and dwarf tobacco plants grow in an informal mass between paving and shingle; red busy lizzies and blue ageratum complement the shades of pots in a splash of co-ordinating boldness and primulas bring a more unusual lilac shade. Where a taller highpoint is needed foxgloves tower in groups and the deep cobalt blooms of the Blue Mountain Lupin echo their clusters of exotic-looking florets opening almost individually. Although a native of the Mediterranean, this plant seems to capture the mood perfectly....

Shapes, colours and textures confer symbolism, mystery, and secrecy. New thoughts and ideas abound. A sense of drama issues from the garden as theatre. These themes are taken up by ourselves and other designers who have been fascinated by the enigma of China and the wider ideas of Oriental style, whether the mood is complete absorption of the theme or hints of the influence of a different way of thinking.

This is not a final statement, but only a beginning, for many possibilities lie in attempting to create 'more or less new form, in terms of one's own taste and time'—and, of course, times change. The contemplation of China is conducive to a philosophical frame of mind. The belief in the desirability of harmony between man and the natural world is tempered by a humble recognition of the insignificance of every human existence; our life represents a fleeting moment. But the Chinese belief does not imply that we should sit back and accept our fate, feeling powerless to make any worthwhile contribution. Our striving to create something new, to open our minds to previously unconsidered ideas, constantly to improve on previous efforts with which one can never quite feel satisfied helps to justify our existence while it lasts.

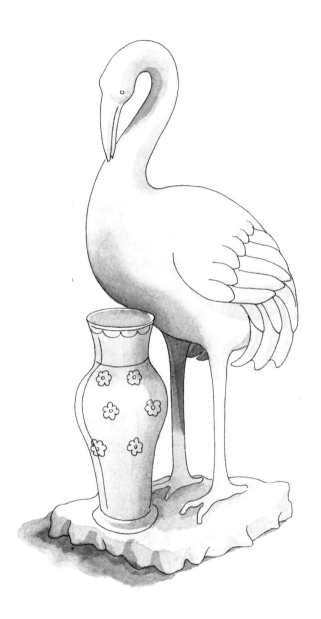

A simple bird figure with ornamental vase.

43 At Breezewood, dense,
rounded mounds of plants lead
the eye to the contrasting
geometric shapes of a tall temple
or pagoda building

44 Rocks bordering a lake at
Breezewood, and set in pebbles
and shingle to create a path with
overtones of Japanese as well as
Chinese influence

First seen over south-west houses,
Fine, fine as a jade hook;
Later reflected on a north-east porch,
Soft, soft like a moth eyebrow.
Moth eyebrows screened by pearl grilles,
Jade hooks set apart by silken windows.

Admiring the Moon From the West
City Gate

45 Small garden with a hint of Oriental style conveyed by plants in pots and displayed individually, textured ground surface and shape of woodwork designs

46 Not a Chinese garden, but Chinese influence in the sparing use of plants with strong form, and shape of the bridge and pebbles used as decoration

Five peach trees in the garden
And one is blooming early.
After two or three fine spring months
Windswept flurries of petals fall on the west house.

The Road is Hard, Four Poems

47 Group of Chinese decorated
earthenware stools contrasts with
textures of stone and plant

48 A sense of mystery: Chinese
urn with swirling dragon
decoration half-hidden amongst
plants and pebbles

THE REALIZATION

For anyone wishing to make a garden inspired by the Chinese style, it should not be difficult to find the basic building materials, nor to locate plants that are either found in Chinese gardens or lend themselves well to the theme. When it comes to accessories, it is becoming easier to obtain pots and statues made in China, as we have shown, but original and attractive timberwork is unavailable from retailers.

In any case, we felt that it would be entirely appropriate to commission new, original designs that would be seen publicly for the first time and would be approached in the same spirit as the garden itself—by echoing the Chinese theme without trying to be replicas of actual pieces.

Having worked with *Practical Woodworking* magazine before, we knew that editor Alan Mitchell would be in sympathy with our ideas and would help to convey them to potential designers, inspiring them to research Chinese style and then translate some of its 'feel' to work which would be entirely appropriate for current taste—with just a touch of the theatrical being distinctly welcome.

At the time of conceiving and making the pieces, all the designers in question were studying at Rycotewood College in Oxfordshire under course tutor Chris Simpson. They already had a good deal of knowledge and experience in woodworking and were finishing their training at an establishment which has built up a good reputation for practical yet innovative work.

All the designs illustrated here could be made by the keen home woodworker who has suitable space and equipment. Alternatively, they could be commissioned from a carpenter or furniture maker, in order to enjoy the benefit of an original design without an exclusive price tag. The woodwork items (all in hardwood) are the bridge which formed the centrepiece of the garden, with its simple, solid design lightened by clever decorative details; a set of planters based on the traditional Chinese urn stand; an elegant small table and a chair which is both practical (and comfortable) and visually appealing. Each piece was conceived by a different designer, but all worked with the same ideas in mind, and so each blends surprisingly well with the others.

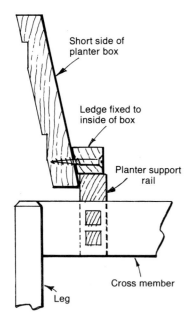

Short side of
planter box

Ledge fixed to
inside of box

Planter support
rail

Cross member

Leg

Three planters in the style of urn stands

After studying Chinese architecture, both past and present, designer Philip Chandler was struck by the fact that they manage to combine simple construction and an ornate appearance. It is these two seemingly contradictory qualities that he wanted to develop, and the result was a set of planters in the form of traditional urn stands, varying in height.

The construction is not only kept simple, but also avoids a reliance on glue, increasing suitability for outdoor use. Mortise and tenon joints are used throughout in the framework of the stand and, to add to the strength and reliability of these joints, the mortises are splayed and wedges driven into the ends of the tenons. In effect this turns the tenon into a dovetail shape which cannot be pulled apart even if the waterproof glue deteriorates in time.

The plant container which sits on top of the framework is assembled using compound mitres fitted with loose tongues. The sides are then held together using galvanized metal strips which are bolted to the timber sides. To further protect the timber from rot, there is an internal container made from galvanized sheet metal.

The making process

First, a cutting list for the timber should be assembled, giving both sawn and finished dimensions. For the sawn sizes allowance should be made for 25mm on the length and 4 to 5mm in width and thickness for planing and thicknessing. All pieces should then be cut to their sawn sizes, and the components planed square, face and edge and cut to finished length.

Next, all the mortises are marked out and cut, then the tenons (this can be carrried out with a radial arm saw to cut the shoulders, with the waste being removed on a bandsaw). Splay the mortises slightly to allow the tenons to form a dovetail when wedged, and assemble the base framework using wedges and waterproof glue.

Cut compound mitres to the plant tub sides, then cut grooves in the mitred faces of the tub sides with a biscuit jointer for the loose tongues. Grooves to 'house' the galvanized metal straps can now be cut on the outside of the tub sides using a spindle moulder fitted with a cutter block. The tub should be assembled with the loose tongues, and then secured with the galvanized straps which are bolted on through the sides. Clean up the tubs before applying two coats of black wood stain.

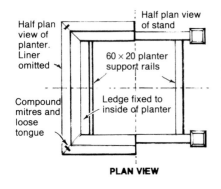

Half plan
view of
planter.
Liner
omitted

Half plan view
of stand

60 × 20 planter
support rails

Compound
mitres and
loose
tongue

Ledge fixed to
inside of planter

PLAN VIEW

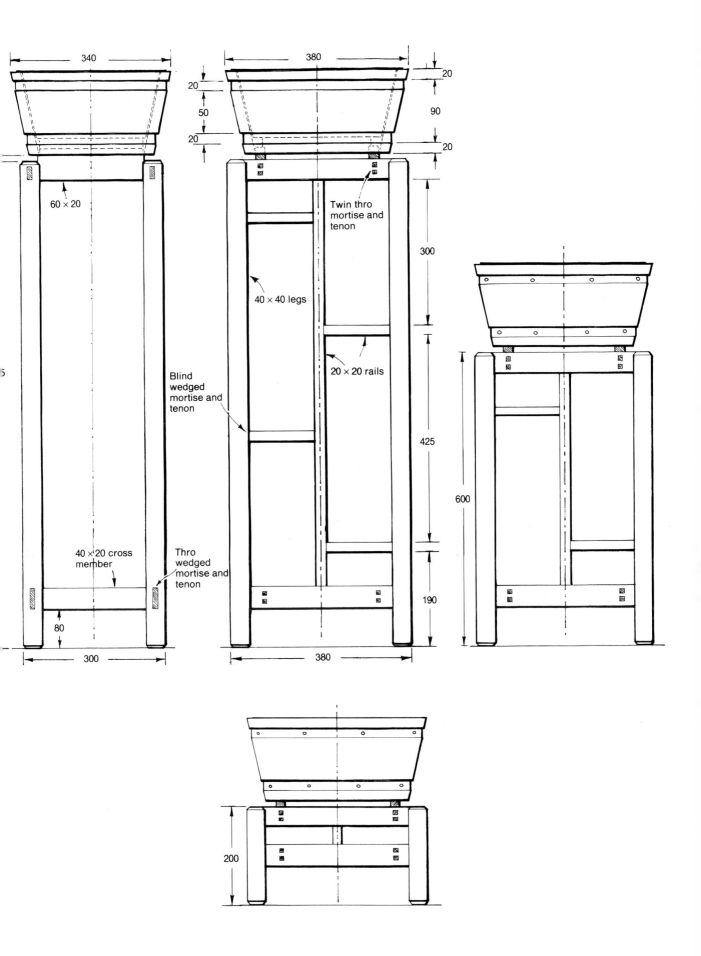

340

380

20

20

50

90

20

20

60 × 20

Twin thro
mortise and
tenon

300

40 × 40 legs

Blind
wedged
mortise and
tenon

20 × 20 rails

425

600

40 × 20 cross
member

Thro
wedged
mortise and
tenon

190

80

300

380

200

The Table

The idea of a Chinese puzzle interested designer Robert Reddyhof. He combined a desire for clean simplicity with echoes of authentic Chinese style—especially the characters of calligraphy and the construction of traditional Chinese temple roofs where lintels continue past the supporting post in a cantilever manner.

The design of the supporting structure for the table employs basic mortise and tenon construction, but the tenon continues through and past the mortise and when wedged povides a strong joint, reinforced by damp conditions, in a pattern recalling Chinese characters. These extended tenons suggest the means of attaching the table top—dispensing with side rails the top itself provides the rigidity. The leg tenons fit through mortises in both the end rails and the top, which when wedged gives the whole structure strength and stability.

The making process

All mortises—other than those in the top which are chopped by hand—are cut with the mortising machine. Tenons are cut carefully by handsaw, and tenon saw. The profiles of the rails and stretcher tenons are realized by marking with a template, roughly cutting by bandsaw, followed by internally ground gouge and finishing with sandpaper wrapped around a piece of dowelling. The same profile can be achieved on the end of the planks forming the table, by setting the blade of the sliding table circular saw to 45°. The face of the cut is then made concave by roughing out with a carver's gouge followed by a round-bottomed wooden plane, and finished again by sandpaper wrapped around dowelling. For wedging the tenons, ebony is used, relating to the black finish used elsewhere in the design.

The use of both natural wood and black finish is an attempt to represent the notion of contrast between positive and negative—yin and yang. Their identity is understood by contrast, hence each component is adjacent to its opposing colour, and the use of complementary coloured dowelling, in addition to providing a decorative detail, is an extension of this motif.

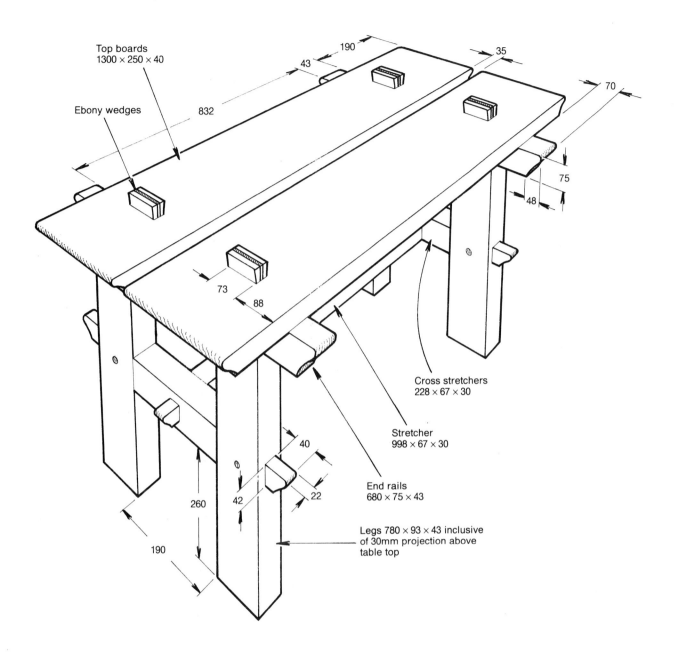

Top boards
1300 × 250 × 40

Ebony wedges

832

190

43

35

70

75

48

73

88

Cross stretchers
228 × 67 × 30

Stretcher
998 × 67 × 30

End rails
680 × 75 × 43

Legs 780 × 93 × 43 inclusive
of 30mm projection above
table top

40

42

22

260

190

The Chairs

In working on the chairs, designer Graham Morris took the view that it was not his aim to establish a direct influence of Chinese design but rather to show the designer's interpretation with a Chinese influence. The chairs are intended not only to be functional, but also to provide interest and visual appeal as pleasing objects in their own right. The final design is simple but attractive with the use of sharp and gentle curves together with the play on space and lines with interlaced detail for the back. It picks up, too, the distinctive curved shapes of the ends of the table cross rails as well as the black finish normally associated with Chinese lacquer work. The lattice back support is also reminiscent of Chinese calligraphy.

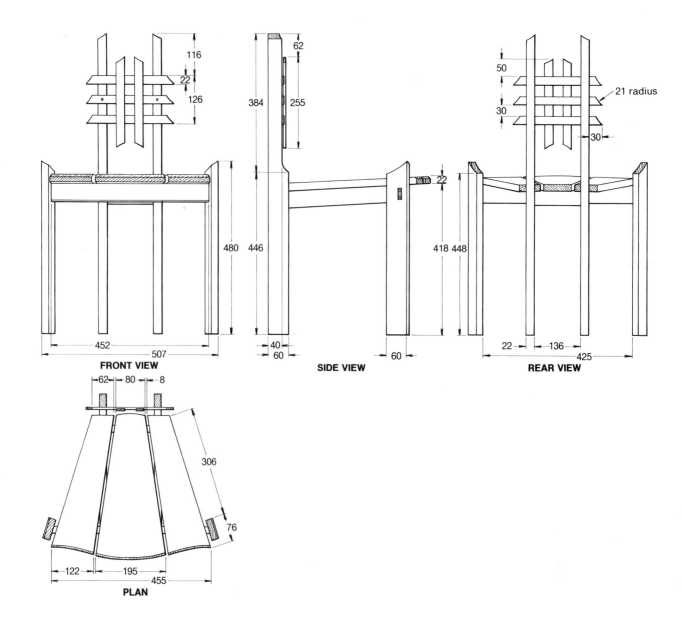

FRONT VIEW

SIDE VIEW

REAR VIEW

PLAN

The making process

First, the material should be prepared to size. Soraya could be used, or a more durable timber such as iroko, teak or oak. Accurate jigs of the various shapes are then drawn out to make full-size templates of the components. These are fitted with locating fences to align the shape quickly in the correct position on the work either to trace around or to cut from. The waste of each shape component is then cut away, slightly oversize, to allow accurate trimming with a router using a following roller bearing off the template to produce a duplicate profile. Each seat segment together with the shaped front and rear legs is treated in a similar fashion working from the squared components.

When each member is prepared to size, the pieces can be marked out and jointed. The important joints, the cross rails where they fix into the legs at the front and rear, are mortise and tenons and secured with pegs or twin decorative wedges.

The cross rails tenoned into the rear legs require an angled shoulder as the seat segments are slightly angled back to provide comfort. Where the cross rails meet the front rail a similar clean angled shoulder is cut and fixed with a double dowel joint. The front rail in turn is fitted into an oblique mortise in the angled front leg and secured with wedges. This is undertaken by fitting the front leg in a cradle jig held at the corresponding angle in the mortising machine. The tenons are cut on the bandsaw using the fence to ensure the correct width of tenon. The sub-frame is then assembled and the spacing rail fitted between the two cross rails with fixing dowels inserted into the end grain.

The chair frame can then be prepared for assembly by cleaning up the mouldings and chamfering the edges. Now it can be glued up and all joints checked for squareness. Whilst the chair is drying, the back rest can be jointed with cross halvings where the pieces cross forming an intricate lattice pattern. However, the two vertical members are slightly raised and curved along the length to take the shape and support the back muscles either side of the spine. The ends echo the shape used on the top of the rear legs; when they have been shaped, the edges are chamfered and cleaned ready for glueing.

The three individual seat segment edges are softened with a chamfer and fixed to the sub-frame by screwing up from beneath. Each segment should be aligned to allow the gently curved shape to flow, whilst ensuring even spacing between the segments. The back rest is centrally mounted with screws to the rear legs. Finally, the back and seat segments are treated with a clear wood preservative whilst the chair frame is treated with a coloured wood finish, giving an ebonized effect.

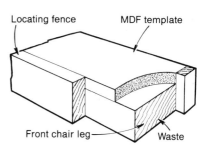

ROUTER PROFILE JIG

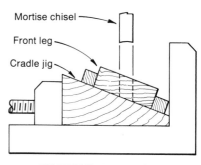

MORTISING AT AN ANGLE

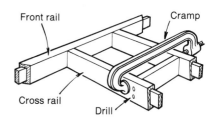

SUB-FRAME ASSEMBLY

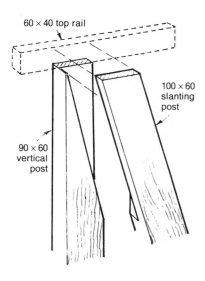

60 × 40 top rail

100 × 60 slanting post

90 × 60 vertical post

The Bridge

The Chinese design of bridges, fences and gates is one of logical and functional mechanics, with a very old decorative style that has been modified gradually by cultural developments over the centuries. Timothy Boyle's design for a bridge draws upon these Chinese elements and yet can be perfectly at home in a modern Western garden that is Chinese-inspired.

In order to incorporate rigidity with a simple form, the two main beams of the span and the beams supporting the steps are held in triangulation by the upright posts and their side braces. The other components are then arranged in such a way that the spaces between the parts are all related in some way, whether this is echoing the triangular features of the main posts and braces, the parallel rails or the triangular ends and scallop detailing. Further strength to the structure is also provided by the four cross beams which serve to make the bridge more rigid and counter any lateral movement.These main components are all bolted together as this provides great strength to connecting timbers without the problems often encountered in conventional joints used in outdoor projects.

The making process

The first step is to convert hardwood boards to suitable sizes for the bridge components, making allowances for planing and thicknessing to the finished sizes. Also when cutting to length it is necessary to make allowances on lengths of components that would need trimming after initial assembly, such as the sloping posts which must be levelled with the ground at one end and trimmed flush with the top rail at the other.

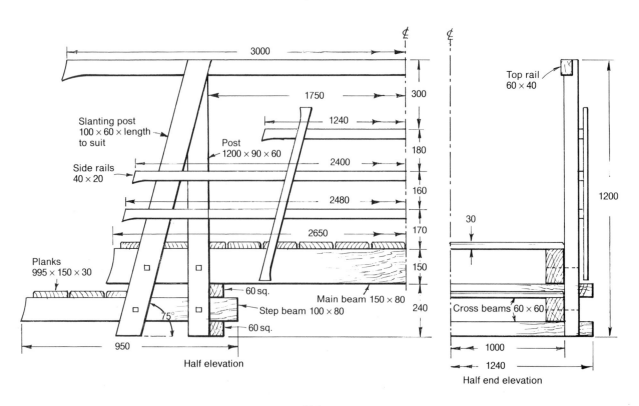

3000

1750

300

Slanting post
100 × 60 × length
to suit

1240

Post
1200 × 90 × 60

180

Side rails
40 × 20

2400

2480

160

2650

170

Planks
995 × 150 × 30

150

60 sq.

Step beam 100 × 80

Main beam 150 × 80

75°

60 sq.

240

950

Half elevation

Top rail
60 × 40

30

1200

Cross beams 60 × 60

1000

1240

Half end elevation

116

Construction is designed to be as simple as possible so that the bridge can be assembled in situ in the garden, using coachscrews. One aspect of the bridge construction, however, which is best undertaken as a pre-assembly is the A-section triangular supports of the vertical and slanting posts. These meet in an angular halving type joint which also accommodates the top rail.

Having established the positions of these two posts on the step and main beams, glue them together with a waterproof glue. The joint can be further reinforced by screwing or dowelling through from the slanting post into the vertical. Screws can be concealed with wooden plugs.

For shaping the ends of the beams and rails, it is necessary to make up templates to ensure that there is an exact repetition of shaping. Also experiment with the curves on the scalloped ends to ensure they are correct before shaping. As an alternative to cutting the decorative side rails from solid timber, an extra piece could be glued at the ends to increase the width so that the end detail may be cut from this to flow back into the straight lines of the middle parts of the rails.

Coachscrews are used to secure the main components and also to secure the cross beams. (Holes must be pre-drilled for these.) Other components such as the foot boards and side rails are held in place with screws. Countersink the screw holes so that after all trial assemblies and dismantling to finish, the bridge can be permanently reassembled and the holes plugged with matching timber dowels. To finish the bridge, the component parts are given a slight chamfer, then after cleaning they are given several brush coats of either red or black stain finish. This has the effect of giving an ebonized type finish with good preservative qualities.

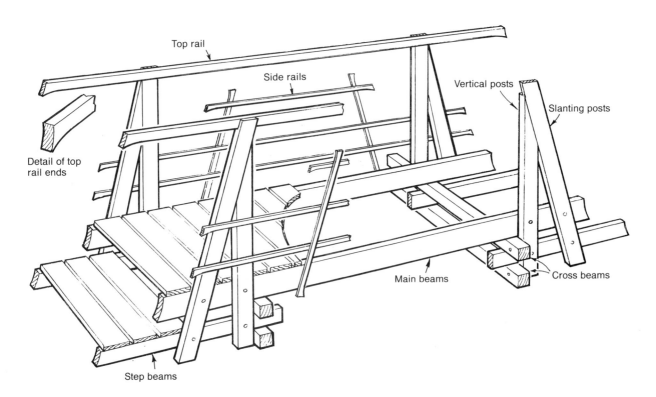

The Rocks

In order to achieve the look of Chinese water-worn limestone, sculptor Malcolm Pollard took several large pieces of British tufa rock—a porous stone that could be almost reformed to create a different look entirely....

Malcolm Pollard's work has been in creative decorative functional items like seats, pots and urns, and in fashioning restoration of decaying ornamental stonework, as well as sculpting as a fine art. He has long had a fascination for Chinese art, sculpture, gardens and philosophy and has studied carefully the Oriental approach to using and arranging rock—its significance, its symbolism, its deeper meanings, as well as its visual impact. Who better then to create the desired impression of Chinese garden style?

The large rocks were first manhandled into position to form groups, carefully arranged so that they would look balanced and seem comfortable—a blend of taller, craggy, more vertical shapes and low, ground-hugging pieces. Some were not sufficiently large to have the desired impact, and so two rocks would be placed plainly together and then the soft surface was chipped with a mason's hammer. Chippings and dust were then pummelled into the crevice between the two pieces, so that eventually the impression was created of one really large piece instead of two smaller. The surfaces of all the rocks were then hammered and chipped painstakingly, until they began to take on something of that lunar quality so distinctive of Chinese water-worn rock.

The now dust-covered rocks were hosed down with water to reveal the finished surface, but the colour was still too stark and so the finishing touch is a light brush over the entire surface with a very simple solution—muddy water. This is readily absorbed by the porous stone and so makes a permanent and effective colourant.

The Pots and Statues

Beautiful objects that have actually been imported from China will help to lend the garden a sense of Oriental mystery and a touch of authenticity. High fired glazed earthenware planters are now widely imported to Europe from the YiXing Pottery in Jiangsu Province, China. They are still made to traditional designs and finished in slip sculptured decoration—often exquisitely ornate, especially on large urns—or the blue 'Chun' glaze (meaning sky after rain). Equally traditional, but slightly less sophisticated in their finish, are Guangdong pots from South China.

Replicas of the terracotta warriors are not the only form of large sculpture that is available in the West. The Tianjin works is situated in Chiu Yang County, Hebei Province, Northern China and specializes in sculptures made from white and black marble and from granite, as well as wood carvings of ancient figures. Indeed, all are taken from originals created centuries ago and reflect ancient Chinese culture and religion.

The main agent for both Britain and Europe for Chinese pots and statues is Snapdragon—founded by potter Brian Hamilton who went to China to seek inspiration for his own work and instead fell in love with theirs.

Suppliers of materials for Chinese style gardens

Rocks, pebbles and stone chippings:
Border Stone,
Middletown Quarry,
Middletown,
Near Welshpool,
Powys SY21 8DJ

Pots and statues:
Snapdragon,
268 Lee High Road,
Lewisham,
London SE13

Original sculpture:
Malcolm Pollard,
42 East Park Parade,
Northampton,
Northants.

**Corinium Paving
(and other paving and walling):**
Bradstone Garden Products,
ECC Quarries Ltd,
Okus,
Swindon,
Wilts SN1 4JJ

Bricks:
Redland Bricks Ltd.,
Redland House,
Reigate,
Surrey RH2 0SJ

Pond equipment:
Stapeley Water Gardens,
London Road,
Nantwich,
Cheshire CW5 7LH

Captions to colour photographs

Further information on some of the colour illustrations

3 Courtyard garden at Hei Long Tan Kunming, framed by moongate with peach blossom decoration. The courtyard is part of the house complex rather than the separate, more informal garden area, but this very appealing formal arrangement seems to create a garden in itself. The appeal lies partly in the obvious artistry, care and attention to detail essential to its creation and maintenance.

4 & 19 Windows in a classical garden at Suzhou. The windows themselves can be appreciated for their elegant design and skilful construction; their role is to provide contrast with the solid wall and frame a 'picture' of the view beyond.

5 Ceramic bamboo stems at Qingympu Garden, Nanchuang. Contrast, colour, texture, form . . . art imitating nature and the artist adding imagination to inspiration.

14 The Garden of the Humble Administrator, Suzhou. The earthenware tables and stools are balanced perfectly in size and shape by huge, magnificently rounded azaleas, which echo the circular theme and introduce vivid colour contrast.

16 & 18 Latticed windows at Liu Yuan—the Lingering Garden—Suzhou. The delicate tracery of lattice work invites the viewer to look closely, then beyond, to see through half-closed eyes a kaleidoscope of strong black line designs and soft, green foliage or grey, mysterious rocks.

20 Pots of primulas and calceolarias on an open lattice window, Tanghua Temple. The effect is not only decorative, but also adds drama to the view of the garden beyond—an idea that could happily transfer almost exactly to a Western garden.

21 Water-worn rock in the Garden of Joy at Yi-Yuan, Suzhou. The rock is appreciated for its shape and its infinitely textured and punctured surface. Water-worn limestone is traditionally the most prized form of rock for Chinese gardens—the more worn and complicated in shape the better.

22 Water-carved rocks in the Garden of the Fisherman, Wang Shi Yuan, Suzhou. The rocks are not a part of some ornamental feature—they are the feature itself, the focus of attention and contemplation of their form, their texture and their arrangement as well as the symbolism of the might of nature in the form of mountains—the home of the Gods.

23 Arrangement of stones in the great garden of the Mosque at Da Qing Zhen Shi, Xi'An. The stone is arranged to be viewed and contemplated from all around as an object of beauty in its own right.

24 The dramatic stems of *Phyllostachys pubescens* at the Hangzou Botanical Garden create a glade where dappled sunlight enhances the contrast of colour and textures.

25 Hundreds of varieties of bamboo are grown in China. In this ornamental form at Canton there is beauty not only in striking contrasts of colour but the fragility of leaves against the strong, solid stem and the 'painted' lines seem reminiscent of the brush strokes of Chinese calligraphy.

26, 27, 28 Designs in the surface of paved areas are created by coloured pebbles and serve to define different areas of the garden with different mood, character or use. The imagery of animals, birds and insects is frequently the basis for the design.

29 The bridge is decorated by a row of pots containing variegated ivies (easily available as pot plants), and a group of foxgloves makes an effective focal point close by. Even familiar plants such as these can lend themselves to a garden with Chinese style, making it more lush and perhaps more suited to Western taste.

30 This life-size replica of a standing warrior from the tomb of Shihuang-Di was made in China and became the first of its kind to be imported to Britain, especially for the Chinese Puzzle Garden. It is made in the same local grey clay as the originals centuries ago and its uniform details denote some form of rank. The grey is effectively offset by a specimen of *Acer palmatum* Burgundy Glow and pots of primulas very similar to those shown in the window decoration in a Chinese garden (illustration No. 20).

31 Images of China combine in a Western garden. The striking red and black ornamental bridge leads to ponds overlooked by Chinese white marble geese. Rock and bamboo create a 'miniature landscape' in one corner and the small, half-hidden figure of a warrior is echoed by the focal point—a life-size replica of a terracotta warrior from the ancient tomb of Shihuang-Di.

32 The chair was designed as one of a set by Graham Morris and—like all the timberwork items—was inspired by aspects of traditional Chinese design and art rather than seeking to imitate it in a repetitive but lifeless form. The chair incorporates quite deliberate contrasts in shape and colour in keeping with the philosophy of yin and yang.

33 The set of three planters designed by Philip Chandler is based on the concept of the elegant Chinese urn stand. It is the more effective for the variation in heights and the plants—which although simple, familiar flowers highlight the colour scheme, especially the red Impatiens (busy lizzie) in the tallest urn.

34 A stunning Chinese earthenware pot can look very dramatic when planted with a tall, striking specimen plant with elegant shape. However, sometimes it is equally effective to keep the plants low and simple—as with this Ageratum—and let the shape, form and smooth, reflective glaze of the pot itself take starring role against a sympathetic backdrop.

35 The lushness of this combination of plants in both colour and form is Western rather than Chinese in its style. This is perhaps one of the secrets of translating the style of the original into a form appropriate to one's own taste and time, as suggested by Farrer. It is not a copy of the original, neither is it a travesty, however, since the spirit of appreciation of nature and the beauty of each plant in its own right is still an underlying philosophy.

36 This overall picture of the Chinese Puzzle Garden shows clearly the shape of the pools, which appear as though they might interlock, as well as illustrating the themes of colour, shape and texture of the garden as a whole.

37 Tall, bushy Photinia with its glossy green and red leaves provides a background to a lilac coloured rhododendron, which leads downward in the composition to the darker shade of primulas. The lilac is hinted at again in the hosta flowers and flows through to stronger deep blue of the Blue Mountain Lupin.

38 The pair of white marble geese are hand-carved at the Tianjin Stone works in China; these, together with figures such as ducks and lions, are becoming more widely available in Europe.

39 Tufa rocks arranged to create pleasing formations, sculpted and weathered echo the look of Chinese water-worn rocks. Here they are effectively offset by plants of Lupinus varius, the Blue Mountain Lupin grown from seed by Mr Fothergills. A native of Israel, this attractive and unusual lupin is grown in cooler climates as an annual.

40 An interpretation of the Oriental style by designer Steve Prescott (Telegraph Garden, Chelsea Show). The design of both the garden and the pagoda (by Andrew Crace) are modern in feel, with clean lines and warm colours. They are inspired as much perhaps by Japan as China, and incorporate shades of both styles. The line of the brick wall and zig-zag path; the decorative low fence; the roof of the pagoda and its elegant furniture; the planting chosen for both colour and texture—and architectural form.

42, 43, 44 An American interpretation of Chinese style: Breezewood Garden is near Baltimore, Maryland. It is privately owned, and created by Mr Alexander Griswold, a dealer in Oriental art.

45 The Oriental look of this small courtyard garden is achieved by the decorative ground surface of Bradstone Corinium paving—each slab with a squared or circular mosaic design—the use of plants including colourful hydrangeas with specimen pine, rhododendron, *Acer palmatum* and *Clematis montana* 'Rubens' (in corner of wall) and the timber bridge and screens designed by Ashley Cartwright for *Practical Woodworking* magazine.

46 Ashley Cartwright's bridge is reflected in the water of a simple rectangular pool with striking aquatic plants and a surround of Corinium paving leading to areas of stone chippings and Quartered Set pavers decorated with arrangements of pebbles. Plants are used sparingly; the bearded iris beside the bridge provides a focal point of colour and strong vertical shape.

47 The decorated earthenware stools are as much ornamental as functional. Their arrangement is deliberate and they are echoed by a Chinese pot with dragon decoration; the Cornus growing in it has light, silvery variegated foliage—again the contrast of colour and texture. The backdrop of slatted timber screen with plants of *Acer palmatum* has the feeling of bamboo stems and leaf forms.

48 The shape of the large urn is echoed in the circular design of Corinium paving and its colours are enhanced by a background of warm brown and buff bricks and golden variegated dwarf bamboo.

Acknowledgements

The authors and publishers would like to thank the following: Dick Spelman and his colleagues at the Halifax Building Society, for whom the Chinese Puzzle Garden was created; Alan Mitchell, *Practical Woodworking* magazine and Rycotewood College; His Excellency the Ambassador for China and members of his staff for their assistance; Jeff Fothergill and his staff at Mr Fothergill's seeds (especially Ann Loads) and Ray Waite for their help with plants.

Thanks to the following photographers and organizations for supplying the photographs used in the book on the following pages: Heather Angel/Biofotos 14, 15, 18, 27, 34, 39, 42–3, 46 above and below, 47, 50, 54, 55 left and right, 58, 59, 62, 63 above and below; Cement and Concrete Association 102; Derek Fell 94, 98, 99; Derek Goard 66, 67, 70, 71, 74, 75, 78, 79, 82, 83, 86, 87, 90, 91, 103, 106, 107; An Keren/Xinhua News Agency 22 and 23 above; Victoria and Albert Museum 10–11, 26; Wang Hui/Xinhua News Agency 31; Xinhua News Agency 7, 21, 22, 23 above and below, 30 above and below, 31, 32; Zhang Shenming/Xinhua News Agency 7; Zhang Shuyhan/Xinhua News Agency 32.

Particular thanks go to Michelle Ross for the line illustrations and to Julian Holland for the book's design. The construction diagrams at the end of the book are published courtesy of *Practical Woodworking*, and the index is by Maureen Webley.

On visiting a Taoist Master; Quiet Night Thoughts; Letter to His Two Small Children; Longing; Three, Five, Seven Words by Li Po and Nine Short Songs: Wandering Breezes and The Ballad of the Ancient Cypress by Tu Fu from *Li Po and Tu Fu* translated by Arthur Cooper (Penguin Classics 1973) copyright © Arthur Cooper, 1973. All other poems from *New Songs from a Jade Terrace* translated by Anne M. Birrell (George Allen & Unwin 1982) copyright © Anne M. Birrell, 1982.

Special thanks to all the students of Rycotewood who participated in the project, especially those whose work is illustrated. The designs remain their copyright as follows: Bridge design © Timothy Boyle; Planters design © Philip Chandler; Table design © Robert Reddyhof; Chair design © Graham Morris.

Index